The Choc

Story by June Melser
Illustrations by Robyn Belton

"M-m-m-m-m-m-m-m!"
said Grandma.

"M-m-m-m-m!"
said Grandpa.

"Mmm-mmm!"
said Mom.

4

"Mmm!"
said Dad.

5

"M-m-m-m-m-m-m-m-m-m-m-m-m-m!"

said Baby.

6

It's all gone!

"More!   More!   More!"
they said.